About the Author

Paula Guildea lives in County Dublin. She holds a BA degree, a Higher Diploma in Further Education, and an MA in Creative Writing. She teaches ESOL and creative writing. Paula's novel *Want* was released in February 2024. She also writes short stories, with work published in various e-magazines and writing journals. In addition, her play titled *Plucked* will be showcased in Smock Alley next year. She is currently working on a manuscript titled *WoodSky*.

Deliberately Yours

Paula Guildea

Deliberately Yours

Vanguard Press

VANGUARD PAPERBACK

© Copyright 2025
Paula Guildea

The right of Paula Guildea to be identified as author of
this work has been asserted by her in accordance with the
Copyright, Designs and Patents Act 1988.

All Rights Reserved

No reproduction, copy or transmission of this publication
may be made without written permission.
No paragraph of this publication may be reproduced,
copied or transmitted save with the written permission of the publisher, or in
accordance with the provisions
of the Copyright Act 1956 (as amended).

Any person who commits any unauthorised act in relation to this publication
may be liable to criminal prosecution and civil claims for damages.

A CIP catalogue record for this title is available from the British Library.

ISBN 978-1-83671-005-9

This is a work of fiction. Names, characters, businesses, places, events and
incidents are either the products of the author's imagination or used in a
fictitious manner. Any resemblance to actual persons, living or dead, or actual
events is purely coincidental.

*Vanguard Press is an imprint of
Pegasus Elliot Mackenzie Publishers Ltd.*
www.pegasuspublishers.com

First Published in 2025

**Vanguard Press
Sheraton House Castle Park
Cambridge England**

Printed & Bound in Great Britain

Dedication

For My Mum and Dad

Acknowledgements

I would like to offer my deep thanks to the family and friends who happily gave their time to proofread my early efforts and to offer their constructive input on my ways and words. My deepest thanks to Alison O' Grady, whose stunning artwork graces the cover, and inner pages of this book. Your creativity captured the spirit of the poetry more perfectly than I could have imagined. I'm honoured to have your vision as the first thing readers see.

Table of Contents

Harbour Men	13
Moon's View	14
Home Travelling	15
A Paper Bag	17
Sit, Wait.	18
YouMe	20
Pin	21
Face	22
Watercolours	23
Broken	25
The Morning	26
SeaSalt	27
To Go	28
Sweep	31
Before	32
The Afternoon	33
A Lady	34
Plucked	36
Old Times	37
Dead	39
Window	41
SHEET	43
Son 25	44
Field	45
Her And You	46

Harbour Men

An old Irish man
walks his dog, while others
watch him walk,
from their windows.
He views the ocean every day—
A tanned face all year round.
His dogs have changed,
he has not—but for the pace
given each step.
Old Irish men, from old
estates, setting out -
To walk the banks,
along the coastline and under the tunnel.
Up and over.
A light wind easing in every season. Grey hair—
Some, not all, under caps, wisps that flap—
Wool jumpers under anoraks.
They meet and chat and walk along bloomed,
bright or fading petals or
bare tree branches or one sits on a rock.
To watch the water dance—
A stride or a limp or a memory of a stride.

Moon's View

Halfway in the lake,
Thighs submerged, touched just so,
As my soul aligns, and I, complete inertia,
Complex, by -
The murky waters you left behind.

The moon's darkened reflection becomes a
Foreshadowing.
For our pain.
While I need to -
Wash you away…
And yet you remain.
The tide is effortless; I almost float.
I remain too, suspended, mislaid.
In what was.
Stained ubiquitously, a stillness without cause.

I talk, you talk, we both delay.
In this murky water,
adrift on display.
Us -

Home Travelling

Underfoot and a path, sand
Concrete, some tarmac. Musing,
As air strolls with raised hairs.
Pebbles under sole, joined
To memories, or the day's happenings,
Or just the day and a passerby.
An overpass, going under, and the
Sun breaks through the clouds, just
As the river meets the sea. A hand rests on a railing,
While dark patches rest on the skin.
Old brick and new cement, painted over dated
Scribbles left by ghosts whose pens sit in a
Dusty drawer, pushed in half-way.
An old net, now part of the landscape, frayed at the
Gathered hole,
Saltwater between twine that sand-filled slabs have
Gathered from a windstorm.
The hill calls forth a wanderer.

A Paper Bag

Your effort at profundity has me
Catching bubbles as if
They're solid circles and
I'm an enabler—
Of sorts.
A vacuum without suction.
A looped lead has been gnawed away by teeth,
Belonging to a wildness caged by a
Past connection, that leaves the door open an inch or
Two at night.
Your unpainted toenails, fixed between the wood,
Like they were meant to be there.
The soft sole of the skin. Underfoot.
The clammy print lifted,
But remaining as you strut.
Your stuff lays on the table, among words from
Yesterday's conversation.
A crumpled paper bag, and all we had said.
Drying inside.

Sit, Wait.

Dark early evenings
I sit and wait.

Buttoned are the cases,
Crepe paper between the laces.
Folding memories two by two—
Leaving out old fabric, then,
To one side,
Old shoes.
Only essentials,
No heavy baggage by the steps.
A new old path is heaving.
Alone is who I've been, alone is where I rest.
This choice of changing seasons,
Each season, at its best.

YouMe

The impenetrable outline of you
hides what I ache to explore.
Your outline and lines,
not meant to chase -
don't care to embrace,
unable to face,
slow down the pace,
wait… just in case.
I hold myself above pressed.
Were I to let it out-
You'd enhance me,
who I crave to be.
But desire, distance, oh that.

A path—
Alone,
but for the sound of that drop, as it dissolves.
Thereupon, we have a chance.
The tip of my tongue,
and doing stuff around the house, before
I sit down to write.

Pin

Come at me like a needle,
Pinprick,
What a prick, little prick.

Lucky your tongue was beneficial,
Lies, lies, lies,
Hypnotised,
I guess.

Face

Sometimes, I see your face
I do.
And with it our chapter,
Our verse—
Moments I protect so dearly,
A lifetime you'd erase,
Unfazed.
Sometimes.
I want to text your number,
I do,
That's not within our code.
Text = words, syllables-decode.
Then I turn my back.
I can't say I'm, 'Right here waiting,'
Cos truth be known, I'm not-
But,
Like Ross/Rachel, it's never off the table.
Cos, well,
We're still breathing—

Indeed, why bleed. Why not? No labels.

Watercolours

The watercolours of my town
change from day to day, the
voices carrying syllables, that
I'd need to replay. Like an old cassette player,
capturing lyrics on rewind.
The ways in which I used to live,
someone else has left behind.

Brighter colours fill busy streets,
dyed with white and yellow, the old ways
out, new ways in.
And with all this,
I mellow.
A birth no less, a brand new day,
Replace a rainbow with the rain.
The sun can shine and dull again.
These small things will settle.

Broken

I was hoping for a respite
while singing to their tune.
I was wailing in the darkness,
set in harshness, deep in gloom.
I'd been prancing, I'd been dancing,
I'd played fiddle with their truth.
The chambers of conclusion,
From a disingenuous youth.
I'd been wandering the open plains,
the plateau of existence,
I'd failed the many menial tasks—
thrived among the shadowed sparks.
The heaped traumas,
no less, than laboured—
Woke suggestions.
And in the same token,
Everything that's fixed
Inevitably
Gets broken.

The Morning

It is not the clouds that argue
Empty threats to the sun. But
Rather a mood that adjusts us.
Has us, seeking us out.
Waiting for this or waiting for that,
I step not into,
But out of… I
Found a spot and hummed in silence.

SeaSalt

On a sandbed, I
Lay.
Face downwards.
Your cramped handprint on my back.
And yet,
The imprint has darkened.
I can't catch a breath with my airways blocked.
Grit rests where the inner eye makes a bed.
My face shapes as I lift, or am lifted.
Unduly.
Imprinting the sand.

To Go

Time to go,
A time for change,
Reconstruct,
Rearrange.
The wind is calling,
Wild leaves too,
The haunting night,
Light morning dew.
Place of rumination,
Solace laid bare,
Graced hub of silence,
A walk amid air.
Bye to the hometown,
Which peaks still appear,
Delicately traced coast,
Fields I hold dear.
Lone person's den,
Dry-edged rock,
Amongst country zen.
Identity abound,
A soul of old.
A truth of the past,
Traditional sip,
Songs by moonlight.
A wallpaper layer,
A bodhran muffled.
A culture maintained, alas,
And in sight.

No new language to echo,
Vibrate and heave.
No myopia lingering,
As evening thieves.
We traverse, as if
Water, seeking
String gaps.
So now I go,
Now, I must leave.
Moving backwards,
To where ancestors drank tea.
Two chickens, one goat,
Two sets of glazed eyes.
Purring contently, ensconced, by my side.

Sweep

If I could stop breathing desire would float away,
Yet the longing is like a spell. A height.
Some highs are an unreachable distance,
But the stretch is, in itself, the conquest,
The high is a place of tempting bliss.
Yet I want it.
Unfounded and intangible,
Oh, but to the heart a million shattered pieces.
Each separate, in their unwillingness to be whole—
Loved.

Steady sweep and gentle bow, elegance and wonder,
All of this and more I am promised,
But the dagger wound is fresh—
I am light in the belief that it can develop.
So I must let you go, unexplored and with regret.
My morals cry, how deep they have festered.
There would only be healing of remorse,
Once the realisation settled,
That the years divided were too many, far too fast a
Stretch.

Eyes will remain and a subsequent thought will
Endeavour—
To bring contentment; then in a moment still,
It will be over and gone forever.
If I wait for you by the window of another lifetime,
Will you come?
When age is a gift, not a barrier. Don't run, just walk
I will be here. Waiting, for what is something.

Before

Yesterday was spent thinking about things thought
About today.
And in a way, it leads us along.
How without the ocean,
We'd be lost in another wilderness, the noise of
Waves replaced by an unrecognisable hum.
Woven by a graspless intersection hanging loosely
By its edges. Holding onto has become easy for
Some. Humming when it hums,
While on the periphery, planted firmly,
Are blooming flowers. That no one seems to notice.
And the outsiders remain inside, rooted though
Alone.
Youth calls from the beginning and asks if
Experience has filled the void.
Looking towards tattered boots, we can't tell, can't
judge.

The Afternoon

As I enter the afternoon of my life,
It settles like dust on an uneven surface. My night
Is fast approaching, simmering
As if heated skyline on the horizon.
It scares me so.
But it happens to us all.
The shine loses its glow,
The skin fades,
The steps slow.
The thoughts don't flow;
They migrate. Music
Mitigates the stress—the knowing. But
It happens to us all. When youth is the past-
There are no questions left to ask.
As the phoenix rising from the ashes,
Leaves without knowing,
Sails without rowing,
Despairs without showing,
Dances without owing.
In his headspace.

A Lady

There's this woman I know, her elegance holds
Words -
I can only wish to articulate, and I see even through
Scratched lenses,
Bits of me – strands, loose wisps – that move when
She moves. And she allows for that. In a place, I
Would cower. Hunched over, trying to hide inside,
protected by heavy lace layers.
She is a lady, giving her wisdom because where she
takes a seat, people gather.
And that's a beautiful thing.
Wiggling her pen, endlessly.
Her effort is less than ours and theirs.

Plucked

I saw you there, standing by the tree, your hair
Untangled – or so it seemed.
The tree stood high, ripe as the sky, and before the
Clouds, you called through the dye.
Tenderly plucked.
Do you remember the taste? The bliss, the bliss, the
Blissfulness.
Was it an apple tree? Did temptation hover? I was
Unaware.
Plants need space to grow, allowing time to show, if
The formation is set,
Being watered just so—
A job not advised without proper instructions,
How was I to know that I hadn't been nurtured?
I'd been slightly uprooted, replanted un-birthed.
And what happened next was the wind changed,
And it changed direction, leaving you open and
Without protection.
Transfixed till you moved, which left a slant to
Your groove,
So I stepped too, to step,
And in that place, we became rooted.
Lifting the slip up and over your shoulder,
We both became bolder, while you, yes you,
Painted rocks from the beach,
You offered a peach,
And you had one too, and it was in that crazy,
Erratic moment, we knew,
I guess.

Old Times

As the old main street
Fades away, its smelly
Alleys,
Its slow decay,
I move away,
I move away,
Etched out of its unfamiliar way.

Who am I?
Well, who are you?
Long before stained air,
I roved these beaches
Skim the stones.
Shoulder to shoulder/ no room to breathe.
Take a walk, not a soul to see, to sea.
Tranquilities' Heaven,
That's what you stole.
Changing waves brought too many—
Changes.

To be more than annoyance.
A bitter taste, a complete waste, of a very delicate
And wonderfully
Astute.
Mind,
Space. Oh, the arrogance—

Dead

Dead from the neck down.
A full sentence choked in the slippery, extraneous
Pow-wowed exchanged between non-believers as if
They get it.
I have no physical desire for a body,
A mind, maybe, a conversation,
But the imagined softened moments
of a sharing are,
Lost on me.
Salient limits arrive, while an intellectual leap into
Lust even,
Preoccupies their mind,
Your mind but not mine. It is not a decision of the mind,
A hoaxed miscommunication,
The mind forms no circumference,
It is not part of the show,
The audience, or even the ticket sellers.
In life, there are people who succeed
And people who fail. I'm the latter.
Especially in these times of small four walls,
And undusted ornaments.
Clothes on top of others,
Baggy tops and stretchy,
Elasticated sweatpants.
An armchair is their home,
Because they've nowhere to go.
Socks on the floor, two pairs

Both scrunched down from the taking-off process
And left as if two cold Yorkshire puddings.
Cobwebs – an odd one here and there – and
Dirt between the wooden floor joins.
And tears left unwiped.
The hype long gone, replaced by
gnawing, trying to chew the reason away.

Window

The curtains are frayed,
And
In many other ways,
The days are gone
Before,
I've woken up,
The light's brighter shine,
I stand behind,
From hiding, some would say,
But,
It's in a different way.
The world's a hefty place.
No comfort in this seat,
A walkway made from sawdust, with
Nothing underneath.
Laired confusion from a window.
The whole world beats.
And it's a soft, soft touch.
Comply, comply,
I've already said too much.
And beyond that,
People sip on Earl Grey tea.

SHEET

And, there's only you.
When the sheet is pulled back.
Alone.
With words in your head.
The sheet was paper thin.
Only fog left.
Vapour.
Until later.
When those words catch a bus.
With no other passengers.
Sitting on velvet cushioned seats.
With stains.

Son 25

How can I, detail
The unimportance,
Of this quiet moment,
In the future.
You,
I'd hide behind.
If I could – you'd be
Protected.
What you need to know,
Those steps taken,
those moulds
forsaken,
won't harden.
Complete, any part of you.
And,
This heart you have,
Tender, as it is, won't
even be carved in a shape of you…

Field

The flowers champion the field,
hiding from the picker who plucks without thought
of lack,
amused by colour and the incident captured.
Somehow smiling, as each petal,
part of the stem,
begins to wither, already.
And the thought is lost,
and the thinker is never identified,
but the field is forever reshaped.
At a loss, a loose patch, stamped and stood upon,
rootless because of the ruthlessness of a human
hand,
a finger with a ring over moisturised skin.
Green without colour has miles,
an overlay into lighter shades,
but spots of colour that grow in between add to its
beauty,
especially in the wild,
where there aren't any rules.
Red is mixed with mauve and sunshine orange in the
hue.
On higher ground,
the view asks questions about nature and reality,
and how peace can be found in the simplicity of life.
The flowers multiply regardless, snatched for
pleasure, they return, replace and reproduce.
A gift, wrapped and given by mystery, the relative of
stormy skies.

Her And You

Being wild isn't an
exception, with tethering.
Rather, trapped -
With the pain -
Of clipped wings,
A nudge to the names and labels.
Patriarchy – handed down,
Shovel fed by women. Some.
Made of steel, standing alone,
In a field,
Full of Pansies.

www.ingramcontent.com/pod-product-compliance
Lightning Source LLC
Chambersburg PA
CBHW060344080526
44584CB00013B/912